a brilliant uncertai
Dasan Ahanu

a brilliant uncertain rebellion
1st edition
ISBN (Trade pbk.)
978-1-7330502-8-9
Layout and Design: Chris Massenburg

www.dasanahanu.com

Table of Contents

For my fellow artists because you deserve to be seen.
I see you.

Faith: a dodoitsu in concert

A room full of brokenness
stuck on my every word
and at that time I learned how
to superglue hope

A room full of brokenness
together, stuck on my words.
I stood on that stage and saw
a stained-glass window.

3000 Out: an ice-cold intro

Being good at something can bring doubt. I didn't understand it until I found myself struggling to fight it off. I used to hear about imposter syndrome. Before too long I came to know it well. It's a hell of a paranoia. One that knows how to show up at the right moment. Knows how to put you in the wrong state of mind. Knows how to push you to do the work necessary to be who you are, then make you feel like you didn't do anything at all. The only saving grace to imposter syndrome is that when that moment is over, you are still the same brightness you were before you ever wondered if anyone thought it was just a flashlight and angles.

Being good at something comes with perceptions and opinions. So much so that expectation becomes other people's definition of your reality. It's a massive weight you are supposed to be excited to carry because knowing that people care should matter. Nobody thinks about having to navigate the writing of a script that uses your voice but doesn't include it. You're just supposed to deliver the lines and be convincing in your performance. You never get to say "action." "Cut" is a scene ending wish you only get if seen as unworthy of attention. The thing about expectation syndrome is that when the moment is over, people still believe they know something, anything. It doesn't matter that they never took time to understand who you are before, they just continue on ignorant as ever after.

Andre Benjamin allowed us to see him searching. Searching for self, for freedom, for room, for new possibilities, for answers to questions some of us have been afraid to let anyone know that we were asking ourselves. I have always admired it. I was inspired by it way before I ever thought myself an artist. Way before I knew what deciding to be one would do for my life or to it. I watched 3 Stacks push, and push some more. I cheered him on because I felt like he was pushing for all of us. Those who showed the kind of promise worthy of other people's expectations. Those who got ahead of being an imposter by embracing the alien in themselves. We watched him change and it changed us. He

—

claimed ownership of his truth, showed us we could too. It didn't get cheered. It got questioned, sometimes ridiculed. It got judged. He kept on anyway. Dammit, he just kept right on until we got used to it, until we accepted it. That was redemptive and revolutionary. A radical transformation the world is still trying to reconcile with.

When I think of what it means to decide for myself what the markers of my life, art, or career's success is, I think of Andre Benjamin. Still figuring it out, but willing to do so to the fullest extent of any possibility in his mind at any moment he feels like trying. It ain't got to be understood. It ain't got to be appreciated. It ain't even got to be witnessed. It just got to be. That is what I think about when I think of Dre. I think of that beautifully uncertain but necessary rebellion. One that says that my days can be spent attending to the whole of myself, insecurity to ingenuity. It says that I deserve that kind of dedication, that we all deserve it. That the world will learn to appreciate it. They will get used to it, accept it. Either way, it will be.

Expectation is all around us. It's in the faces of lovers, in the voices of supporters, in the confusion of family. It becomes gossip, social media posts, or in some cases, headlines. It becomes the desire for folks to pull us to the side to tell us about all we could be doing. Funny how they never ask what we want to be doing in the first place. In their mind we're only doing what we are because we don't understand what's waiting for us. The direction we are supposed to be headed in is told to us. Like they are some magical map makers we've been waiting to find. The journey to our happiness and success is supposed to be mapped to their satisfaction and not ours. That expectation is a hard thing to escape. It comes with the phone calls we get, the offers thrown at us. It is present in the way folks describe us, introduce us, or sing our praises. It's there, waiting.

I've yet to see expectation improve the quality of someone's life. I've never seen it mend a broken relationship. Never seen it heal wounds. Never seen it bring joy or happiness. I haven't seen anyone thank it for the smile on their face. I haven't seen it given credit for the most impactful moments

—

of a person's life. I haven't seen it hold someone when tears flow and body slumps. I haven't seen it laugh with someone loud and full enough to push pain away another day. It doesn't show up when you're lonely. If it did, you'd still feel the same. It doesn't bring the lost back from the dead. It can't cook dinner. It doesn't know what's good to watch on Netflix. I mean, shouldn't I give not one bit of care about nobody's expectation?

The only happy I can guarantee is the one I go find for myself. The only comfortable I can be is the one I choose. I came to this art for catharsis. It offered me so much more. My commitment to it gave me a new life, but it is a life I plan to live the way I damn well choose.

We dictate this wild ride given to us.

I know because I seen't it.

There is someone who showed us what that looks like. Brilliant, broken, flawed, fabulous, and still figuring it out.

Let's join him.

Let's leave that expectation behind.

Let's be out.

Ground Floor

What else is there for a morning star
but purgatory when the devil
is what your pen is?

When the you that you put on paper
is what earns you accolade,
can you honestly say you didn't
barter your soul for success?

Is crafting your next opus a hell of a rush,
a hell of a problem, or a hell of a gift?

When you can't figure out what to write
do you call on God for an answer
or to bear the blame?

If it leads you back to the words
do you consider yourself forsaken or blessed?

Are you mad you're stuck having to
impress this earth with the way
your voice resonates in verse?

Does the audience have a lust for chaos
or is this just what they expect from the fallen?

Is there redemption when you walk away?

When you don't care about being known
anymore do you call that being saved?

Do you wear white to throw away your
empty journals and pens used to raise damnation
on the lines of the page?

Was there a storm or a rainbow after?

Are you still waiting to see if it was good?

Are you still wondering if it was God?

—

Earth tones are really bruises

What do you do when your joy
tries to choke the life out of you?
When your passion has been crafting
a shank out of your insecurities?
Walks through the breadth of your success
with a grudge.
Waits to catch you in general pop.
Gives you a gut feeling
you ain't worth the acclaim.
How long before you come to wish
nobody knew your name?

How long before you start to believe
that you were destined for this?
Title fights with imposter syndrome.
Your name on the bill
feeling like pay per view.
Do they know how many days you spent
sparring with doubt to be in shape?
How much effort it takes to make weight
feel like purpose?
What a damning reality it is to know
that what you are going through is so unfamiliar
to those in your corner that they
wouldn't know when to throw in the towel.
Just hold them to their eyes
to wipe the tears after you die
achieving.

Isn't expectation a bully that takes
your freedom every lunch period
before you can taste a bit of it?
Dares you to tell somebody.
Ain't nobody gone understand this fear.
Ain't nobody gone grasp this kinda hurt.
How weak will you look, how ungrateful?
Ain't you happy to have folks on your side?
Supporters who will tell the world to let you be,
but only so you can create more of what
makes them care about you

—

in the first place.

What did you actually learn from it all?
That ain't no crippling stance like conviction.
That ain't no burden like notoriety.
That ain't no louder sound made
than when tears fall and
nobody wants responsibility
for the pain.

The South Said It: the game talked back

Lord knows excellence don't get you
no satisfaction.
A complex duality of perseverance,
of pushing through.
Every breakthrough is a benchmark
and a shackle.
Mark of achievement and the
establishment of expectation.

Pushing through is a balancing act,
two sides of perseverance.
Claim of restitution and cause for celebration.
You ain't here without us.
Yo ass don't get to be there without us.
That there acceptance speech ain't nothing
but a damn albatross.

Each benchmark or shackle is
like a gold chain, nigga.
Yeah, wear it with unsolicited opinions
like high fashion.
Dress that doubt up like it ain't
imposter syndrome on dat ass.
Ain't billboard a sign of success and
IOU due on demand?

Achievement and expectation are
the marks of establishment.
That albatross ain't nothing without
your acceptance.
Your success signed an IOU and
Billboard demand it be due now.
God knew winning wouldn't
get you no satisfaction.

Asouthernplayalimerick

There once was an onia that was stank
where folks sipped good and smoked dank
playa tongue had to be slick
hips, lips, and thighs stay thick
and yo car had to ride slab with that paint

Ain't no return for the "G"

They say never forget where you came from.
But nigga,
what if they never knew where you was from
when you was there?

So you show them where you from, right?
My nigga,
they turnt that into a prison and got you out here
a refugee from your own reality.

Now you out here turning opportunities
into vacation spots.
These niggas
ain't marveling at your dexterity, they calling
you back to where they ran you from.

You show folks what freedom look like.
Them niggas
treating your past like ruins, excavating artifacts
for clues to the answers you giving them now.

You modeling all the possibilities of creativity.
Some niggas
still waiting for you to decide to come back
to their expectation like that was ever home.

The Way You Ghazal

remember when her saying, "just tell me the truth"
had you searching for something more appealing than the
truth?

my grandfather woke every morning for biscuits and
coffee. sat with the daily newspaper open searching
for truth.

my sister spent her weekends on a dimly lit dance floor
offering her body to the rhythm in exchange for an escape
from the truth.

pastor channel surfs for conservative news like calling to
the altar unable to recognize that a propagandized penance
is the not the truth.

folks earning their woke by spending hours shaming
dissonance. choir speaking bout the extensiveness of white
lies instead of a Black truth.

they still claiming colorblind because a convenient
humanitarianism means that their privilege ain't got to be
disrupted by an uncomfortable truth.

schools still trying to figure out how to indoctrinate a more
appealing honesty because you can't train obedience by
telling the truth.

but ain't we all looking for a more appealing honesty Slim?
cuz it means we don't have to tell ourselves the truth.

Keep your heart...

Every winter single
is a misery I'm still trying
to get use to

Every summer single
is an exercise in trying to relearn
what warmth feels like

Every in between
reminds me of the roller coaster
I can't escape

The rise and fall
The anticipation
The disappointment
The time spent believing
you're worth it,
reminding yourself your worth it,
but wondering if you'll ever
know what it is
you're worth

Then it's cold all over again
alone all over again
You start
all over again

Tenant Residue

HER said I looked unapproachable.
I said it's 'cause SHE lives in my lap.
HER asked how long we been together.
I said SHE ain't been back home since
SHE told me SHE couldn't get over
the embrace of another man.
HER looked surprised.
I told HER that HER tone didn't
convey HER looking
for a heart or a mind, just a
vacation home to call fun.
SHE lives in my lap as a reminder of
what a sublet desire feels like.
It's why my face displays that there
is no room for temporary occupancy.

———

Hey ya over there!

I once believed I could love
you close from a distance.
Just knew I could protect the
me you were waiting on
by letting you have it out with the
me who scheduled the appointment.
When they say better late than never,
they don't mention how clock ticks
sound like your heart breaking slowly.
Top of the hour looks like smoke rising
from the rubble.
Half past feels like digging through
the landfill.
Quarter til seems like I've made peace
with the decay.
Made a bed out of the fragile of it all.
Laid to rest any idea of restoration.

I made believe I was whole once.
That there weren't parts of me missing.
I smile caulked and devotion spackled
the holes in who I be.
At least the who you saw me try to be.
Happy and attentive were co-conspirators.
The plan was to rob you of any idea that
there was more of my vulnerability
tucked away for a rainy day.
They call it a victimless crime when
you don't know what's happening
and I don't know why I'm doing it,
but the damage is the same.
It's always the same.

I try to believe in the idea that you'll
kiss me moving company useless.
That we can unpack and get rid of these
insecurities on our own.
But we can't.
So now I'm calling on God, you
calling your momma, and

14

our hearts are calling for a
home makeover.
Difference is
that yours is a rebuild.
Mine is an intervention.
A desperate attempt to address
the way I have hoarded
every goodbye, every closed door
in my heart.
Love don't live there anymore because
it was deemed uninhabitable.
So now love resides in a loft apartment
above my ears trying to figure out
what's worse.
That my thoughts make noise
through the night
or that the ground shook when
you made my heartbeat quicken.

I want you to believe in me.
Loan me your optimism.
Just enough for the cleaning
and repairs.
I know it's a risky venture.
I need you to believe it's
worth the possible return
on your investment.
Real estate that can only
appreciate in the way
it values having you
in my life.

A negro speaks of deuces (a rondeau)

you making sad songs, saying it hurt too much
revisiting this and that, talking bout such and such
god tried to tell yo ass the last time
you jumped in the devil's arms right after the last line
caught up the fire you felt from her touch

but you mad at her effort, after y'all chose to love dutch
tugging clothes and shifting bodies, fucking like a clutch
mining her for self-worth like it's something you gone find
and got the nerve to be making sad songs

insecurities had you crippled, looked to her like a crutch
how could it feel so right and get fucked up this much
negro you chose the chaos, ignored all the signs
made your healing her burden, is you out your damn mind?
you blaming her talking bout locking your heart in a hutch
got yourself caught up... but you out here making sad songs

Tell da story right

For every Suzy Skrew there is someone right now
telling anybody who will listen bout how you
can't turn a ho into a housewife.

For every Sasha Thumper there is somebody shaking
their head about how folks should turn to something
other than drugs to ease their pain.

But those men won't accept their responsibility.

Won't admit they the source of both. The statement
and the drugs. The perception and the pain.

Will make the niggas that contributed to the situation
seem like a figment of imagination.

Just keep playing with their invisible friends like
recess ain't never had casualties.

Act like they ain't got shit to do with it.

Ain't that a patriarchal shame?

An Idle Wild

There is a blue-collar paradox
stuck at the bottom of a mine shaft.
It was digging a path to healing,
(you know) doing the work,
when an insecure shift
crumbled the solid understanding all around.
The flicker of an oil lamp,
diminishing oxygen,
and relentless spirit are all it has left.

When I open my mouth
it hopes someone will hear
it scream for help.
Unfortunately,
my heart and mind
are in the business of holdings,
(you know) together and inside.
The higher ups tend to cover it up with
"I'm Good" propaganda.
Credit a damn good PR department
for a good spin.
Makes you forget the corruption.
Makes you ignore a time ticked termination.
This project was never safe in the first place,
but clearances can be bought.
Just bribe any conscientious regulation
by paying attention
to more engaging illusions.

Be it lust, lies,
liquor or liberation,
we learn to turn addiction into
a beautifully dysfunctional distraction.
Make displays of assurance and
confidence a compelling ad campaign.
Get wrapped up so much in spin
that our dizzying avoidance of the truth
makes us believe we savant.
Like confusion is a prophecy.
Like irrational is a long-term relationship.

Like our own hype
is the only embrace that makes sense.
We become trapped.
Can't make it without another fix.
Can't make it believable without a
convicted performance.
Can't make no sense out of the corrupt
of this top down governance
where your brain lays your gut off,
makes your self-doubt work overtime,
and tells the world your heart
was too cowardly to put an end to it all.

You know the tragedy
of this crowning hegemony.
Know that deep inside
are the bastions of syntax and diction.
They have been left gasping for air
because the world values
ends over means.
You want a happy ending.
The world wants a more engaging headliner,
a more salacious desperation.
Ain't no greater entertainment
than the eloquent angst
of an artist who has lost whole work crews
and been perched on a throne atop ruins.

———

So-lo (Blackout)
*from "So-lo(reprise)" on Frank Ocean's Blonde

I can see an ant
So low that
I just go "eh"

admit
another kid shot by the popo
ain't an event no mo'
So low

there's a hole where there once was a logo,
how fitting

I can give a fuck about

winning,

Over
Sayin'
we real persons
I hate that it's like this, and

I
pardon me if I am being insensitive
But darling
my halo it feels like it's bent
So
I pay no attention to it
I feel like

I'm on punishment
Watchin' the end

and, yeah, that shit hurts me

20

Two Dope Boyz at a Bus Stop

I saw a red dodgeball in
an empty sandlot and I
wondered if it was a burial
marker for the last bit of melanated
wide eyed wonder not deemed
worthy of compassion, understanding,
or due process.

I paid the boy at the bus stop $20 to
use his imagination to dig as far as he
could beneath the sand. Now he and
I are both standing here staring at the
lot wondering who we should airbrush on
our t-shirts first.

The city bus pulling up finally disrupted our
mourning. On the side of it was an
ad for almond and soy milk. Funny how
dark things are promoted as better for you
when they are considered white performing.

We both looked at the side of the bus and
then at each other. I shook my head. His shoulders
slumped. He gave me two quarters and a
bar of chocolate. I watched the doors close
behind him.

Now I'm standing here with change unwrapping
candy like I'm trying to resurrect somebody's
black child wondering if I just spent a moment
with God. Wondering if what I just witnessed
was prophecy. Debating if it's true that for every
life lost another affirmation of the pain we are
covered in is born.

The Album Ain't Coming

Our trauma is not a trope. Our lives are more than drama and tragedy. We are more than brokenness for applause or sympathy. We are more than your nostalgia at our expense. You can remember your fondest moments as long as we can remember what it's like to be whole and happy. Our strength is not dismissed for a better storyline. There is no reality show more important than watching our healing. You cannot call our art majestic, allow our demons to cast it crippled, and then rush to add your condemnation to the reviews.

We must be dedicated to the sanctity of all of us. Not to the soundtrack of us. Ain't no satisfaction in knowing you'll type well wishes when we crack, craft think pieces when we falter, or give teary eye memorials if we crumble. Let us find our peace now.

Your awareness of our pain is a short-sighted effort when your expectation is a part of the hurt. It is past time for us to have to fight to be who we are. Bold, flawed but capable, joyous, questioning, assured, insecure, grappling, confident, nuanced, dynamic, still learning, wise, compassionate, angry, brash, laid back, cool, collected, a hot mess, beautiful, beautiful, beautiful, beautiful... whole. Alive.

Prototype for Breakthrough

Where do the beautifully beleaguered
legends reside? Where are the wretched
wonders too masterful to be allowed
to apprentice another way to find happy?
Those who understand what it is like
to become invisible because you're so seen.
Those who know what it's like to build
a playground, be trapped outside it,
but still held accountable for everything
they tear apart inside. Who know what
it is like to have to break into yourself
to fix things. Take me to them. THEM.

Take me to those who trudged their way
through the madness. I want to sit with
those who can tell me stories about coming
out the other side. I want to believe it's possible.
I know they are the only ones who can map
me an optimism I can hold on to.

Cuz don't nobody know what it's like to fight
fires unless they can tell you the smell of smoke.
Unless they can describe the desolate melancholy
of ashes. Can't nobody tell you about building
with no callouses. Can't show you how to enjoy
victory with no battle scars. Can't teach you how
scary truth is unless they have lied enough to shake
earth and crumble rock.

I know about the journey. I want to learn about the
destination.

Let me look into their eyes and know that it's real.

—

23

Letter to Myself

I sometimes find myself
talking to myself like

Dear walking in your purpose
I don't know whether it's admiration
or jealousy
To watch this community see you
treasure
Knowing that I sometimes see you
burden
This thin line between guilt and love
This tug of war between responsibility
and angst
Am I wrong for feeling part scientist,
part god, part toxic origin story?

Dear angst riddled artist
We have endured this long-term relationship
for some time now
Feeling responsible for the folks who fall
into the chasm of disappointment between us
Expectation is a misguided navigator and
it is oh so hard to reconcile when two truths
are so far apart from each other
They see you and feel they have a sense of me
They experience me and wonder if I have
betrayed their sense of you
Wonder if the truth of me is
an illusion of you
All because you keep on being so damn beautiful

Dear Mr. Community Minded
Mister so damn philanthropic
Giving your time, spirit, wisdom, and joy
to any wide-eyed belief in something more
or any pain filled temple seeking escape
But that is not charity in your eyes
Just the possibility that good deeds
are deserved of more work
That more work is the tithes paid

for the blessing of them words
The heaven in that ink
The glory in each smile applauded
hallelujah

Excuse me
Sir
Ole lose yourself in your work
ass boy
We don't talk about the future
We have learned to play our position
I ponder
You act
I worry
You write
I strategize
You anchor these daydreams
to right now
Hammer them into fertile soil
Tie a string to my self doubt
Allow the space between us to become sky
Until the knee bent, hands clasped
praying kite I become
finds freedom
But you
You stand on solid ground
committed to a grassroots effort
in modeling breakthrough

Dammit
You are the extroverted eloquence
this introvert admires from afar
The social butterfly effect of
ancestors past and of
tradition to be made
It's like a hitchhiker's guide
to the galaxy of a page
A novel fantasy you made tangible

I can't stand to not help
but be blown away
To watch this community see you

———

treasure
Knowing that I sometimes see you
burden
This thin line between passion and purpose
This tug of war between mirror and notebook
Am I wrong for feeling part rebel,
part heathen, part ongoing denial
A jealous worry that I am
the night sky that that will
never be as alluring as dawn?

Life of Pan

Purpose is calling
Sounds like Sunday morning
Feels like a mass choir solo
Like exactly what I was waitin' on
Like exactly what I needed to hear
Reminds me that I am here for a reason
And there is a nigga playing a flute in the airport

Freedom is calling
Sounds like a Saturday afternoon
Feels like a family cookout
Like in the midst of familiar is home
Like knowing we in this together is comfort
Reminds me I ain't in this alone
And there is a nigga
playing a flute in the airport

The stage is calling
Sounds like a Friday night
Feels like a parking lot with the homies
Like sitting on chariots talking like gods
Like shawty flew in on a lightning bolt
Reminds us white people love us mythology
For real, there is a nigga playing a flute
in the airport

The mic is calling
Sounds like Tuesday evening
Feels like momma saying eat all your food
Like hard work turned cans into loaves and fish
Like ain't no miracle like magic made
Reminds me how full you can get off of what's possible
Like, yo...
there is a nigga
playing a flute
in the airport

Boarding call
sounds like a Wednesday evening
Feels like a study in the word

———

Like ain't the answers been text on page
Like ain't interpretation changed lives
Reminds me who I can reach with this gift
I mean... there
is a nigga playing
a flute
in the airport

CPSIA information can be obtained
at www.ICGtesting.com
Printed in the USA
JSHW011103240723
45285JS00008B/198